AIR FRYER COOKBOOK WITH PICTURES

Easy and Quick Recipes That You Can Cook Every Day with Your Family. Cooking Together is Fun Family Time.

Keri Fox

TABLE OF CONTENTS

INTRODUCTION

Isn't it incredible that sticking to a healthy diet will help you trim down and keep more of your hard-earned cash in your wallet? You only have to get good at air frying. Regardless of your experience level in the kitchen, this book will be a valuable resource for you. Here you will find recipes for mouthwatering meals that the whole family will love.

An air fryer is a wonderful appliance for the kitchen since it allows you to make delicious food ahead of time without using a lot of oil or fat. As a result, you'll be able to whip up some healthy and tasty meals at home. All of the recipes in this book can be prepared using an air fryer. There is a dish and an occasion in this book for everyone. All three major meals and desserts are covered with a wide range of choices.

You can choose from a variety of nutritious breakfast and dessert items, all of which will make your mouth water. As time goes on, it seems like there aren't many technological advancements that help in the kitchen. Improvements in food quality are within the reach of any home cook because of the availability of new cooking technologies. Air fryers have seen significant growth in sales during the past few years.

A lot of different foods work well when air-fried, which is fantastic news. I have compiled a large number of recipes, all of which feature an image of the final dish. You may decide to purchase an air fryer after trying the recipes in this book. An air fryer is the first truly cutting-edge kitchen gadget in decades. Fry your food in hot, dry air instead of oil to lock in the flavor while creating a crispy exterior.

An air fryer isn't just another kitchen appliance that will end up gathering dust despite its low-key design. In addition to producing nutritious "fried" dishes, baking is another option. This fantastic tool may be used for a wide variety of cooking methods, including grilling, baking, steaming, and stir-frying. In all likelihood, you'll employ it frequently. All of the recipes in this book are healthier and better for you than anything you could make in a deep fryer. These recipes are suitable for use with any brand of air fryer. You may also tweak the temperature and color of any of your air fryer recipes to your liking. Modifying the number of ingredients allows you to make more or fewer servings than the recipe specifies. Let's get this party started!

CHAPTER 1 :
AIR FRYER 101

The Advantages of Using an Air Fryer

In the pursuit of weight loss, an air fryer may be an incredible time-saver and life-changer in the kitchen. Some of the advantages of using an air fryer while dieting are:

1. Minimize fat. Using hot air circulation, air fryers cook food to the same crisp exterior and tender interior as traditional deep fryers, but with far less fat. The air fryer is multifunctional and may be used for other cooking methods besides frying. An air fryer is a great tool for improving the efficiency and taste of whatever cooking method you choose.

2. Quick Turnaround. As a result of the rapid circulation of hot air, most dishes may be prepared in an air fryer in a fraction of the time it would take using conventional cooking methods. As a result, you're going to continue using the book's simple recipes. Want to make sure it's ready? To have a peek, simply slide the basket open. Is it

necessary to rotate the dish during cooking to guarantee uniform browning? You should give the basket a little shake.

3. A smaller amount of clutter. The cleanup process after air-frying is much simpler than after using deep fat. Because one unit is sealed off from the rest, spills are not an issue. The majority of air fryer baskets are nonstick-coated, making cleanup a breeze. You can ditch the dishes and focus on living an active lifestyle. Keep in mind that the air fryer needs to be cleaned and maintained in accordance with the manufacturer's guidelines for safety.

4. Coziness and practicality.If you want to quickly get your kitchen to a roasting hot temperature this summer, try baking with a normal oven. On the other hand, due to their small size, air fryers do not produce nearly as much heat. Some brands even make air fryers that double as pressure cookers, and many versions have settings for baking common foods at the touch of a button. There aren't many things that an air fryer can't make better than a regular oven. The only catch is that the smaller sizes of the units may mean you may need to divide up some recipes into multiple batches. That's easy enough to do, and it might even help you control the portion size when baking cookies or other sweets in bulk.

A recipe for slimming down

To sum up, using an air fryer can help you save a lot of calories and fat. You have to play the numbers game to succeed at weight loss. Once you know how many calories your body typically burns, you can reduce your calorie intake by 500 each day and expect to lose one pound per week. Your BMR can be easily determined with the help of one of the many available internet calculators.

For an even more accurate estimate of your daily caloric expenditure, these services will also take into account your initial body mass index (BMI) and your anticipated levels of physical activity. To lose weight effectively, you need to maintain a baseline metabolic rate that is between 1,800 and 2,200 calories per day. Extreme calorie restriction might disrupt your metabolism and force your body to store fat. Create a target that you know is feasible, secure, and doable. In addition to calorie monitoring, these easily managed methods can help propel your weight loss efforts.

Diets should target fat. Giving that nine calories can be obtained from 1 gram of fat, which is more than twice as many as can be obtained from 1 gram of protein or carbohydrates, paying close attention to the products you use and the fats you employ in cooking is an excellent approach to controlling your calorie intake. However, not all fats are the same. Some are considered heart-healthy because of their involvement in regulating inflammation, such as the monounsaturated fats found in olive oil and almonds. Generally speaking, it's best to limit your intake of saturated fats (abundant in red meat and full-fat dairy products). Most experts agree that trans fats, such as those used in processed meals, should be avoided.

Helpful Kitchen tools

You can use any oven-safe dish, be it glass, metal, or silicone, as long as it fits in the air fryer's basket and doesn't obstruct the hot air vents. Other than your air fryer, you'll need these to make the most of your weight-loss efforts:

1. Kitchen scale: One of the most useful tools in the kitchen is a simple scale for measuring individual servings of food. To determine the true weight of a cut of meat, all you need is a digital scale.
2. Olive oil spray: Instead of using nonstick cooking spray, which could eventually damage your nonstick cookware, consider investing in a spray bottle designed for olive oil instead. To get the best results from air frying, some meals, especially those with a breaded coating, benefit from a light coating of oil first. Avocado oil is great if you want an oil with a subtle flavor.
3. Parchment paper: Use parchment paper, which can be treated with a small layer of silicone to provide a nonstick surface for meals that are too fragile to risk falling through the air fryer's basket openings. If you're using the parchment to line a basket, don't make the mistake of cutting a sheet big enough to fill all the openings (otherwise, air will not circulate properly).
4. Meat thermometer: The only definite method to know if meats are cooked to a safe temperature is to use a meat thermometer, even though the recipes in this book include visual clues to illustrate what your food should look like when it's done.
5. Tongs: Some items require careful turning with tongs, while others can be cooked evenly by merely shaking the basket. Tongs come in handy for this.
6. Don't skimp on protein. Eat plenty of protein. Gaining muscle requires protein, which also helps regulate hunger and keeps your metabolism revved up. However, many protein-rich foods are also heavy in fat, so choose leaner sources like seafood and poultry wherever possible. Also, picturing a healthy portion size can be useful.

Generally speaking, a serving of chicken breast is around the size of your hand or a standard deck of cards.

7. Be careful with carbs. Pay close attention to your carb intake. Carbohydrates serve several purposes in the body, but when dieting, it's helpful to view them as a type of fuel supply that arrives in varying intensities. Sugar and white bread are examples of simple carbs, which the body processes fast yet leaves you feeling hungry after eating. However, complex carbohydrates are similar to premium fuel that your body consumes at a slower rate and hence are preferable. Carbohydrates should come primarily from whole-food sources, including grains, fruits, and vegetables, as they provide a wide variety of additional health benefits and are essential to any sensible weight-control diet.

8. Take in additional fiber and hydration. Fiber, the indigestible portion of plant matter, is found in complex carbohydrates and aids in the regular passage of waste products and intestinal contents. Fiber aids weight loss by keeping you full for longer, which is why it is often recommended for those who are trying to cut calories. Try to get 25 grams of fiber every day. In the meantime, make sure you're getting in at least 8 glasses of water every day; dehydration is a common cause of binge eating.

Using an air fryer and some of these clever eating strategies, you can lighten up your go-to dishes and make weight loss a breeze. Aiming to get your hands dirty? There is a full breakdown of the calories, fat, and protein in each recipe in the following chapters so that you can maintain your diet and fitness routine. Each meal is optimized for use with an air fryer and weight reduction, making healthy eating a breeze. Your air fryer is the key to enjoying delicious food while you work toward a healthier lifestyle.

Chapter 2: Breakfast Recipes

GRANOLA

Serves 4 • Turnaround time: 10 minutes • Total time: 1 hour 10 minutes

Ingredients

- 3 tablespoons canola oil
- 3 tablespoons honey
- ½ teaspoon vanilla extract
- ¼ teaspoon ground cinnamon
- ¼ teaspoon salt
- 1½ cups rolled oats
- ¼ cup pecans or walnuts, coarsely chopped
- ¼ cup raisins or other dried fruit

Method

1. Preheat the air fryer to 250F. The basket of the air fryer should be lined with parchment paper.
2. Combine the oil, honey, vanilla, cinnamon, and salt in a large bowl. Stir until completely smooth. Stir until the oats and nuts are evenly distributed throughout the mixture.

7

3. Evenly distribute the oat mixture on the parchment paper.
4. Cook for one hour in the air fryer or until evenly browned. Remove it from the air fryer and cool it to room temperature. If necessary, break the granola into bite-sized pieces and mix in the raisins.
5. And keep it for up to one week in an airtight jar.

Per ½ cup serving:

330 calories | 5 g protein | 42 g carbohydrates | 17 g fat (1.5 g sat fat) | 4 g fiber

CHERRY-OATMEAL BARS

Serves 12 • Turnaround time: 15 minutes • Total time: 50 minutes + cooling time

Ingredients

- 4 tablespoons unsalted butter
- 1 cup rolled oats
- ½ cup all-purpose flour
- ¼ cup packed light brown sugar
- ¼ teaspoon ground ginger
- ¼ teaspoon kosher salt
- ½ cup all-fruit cherry preserves

Method

1. Preheat the air fryer to 370F. Prep a square baking dish, 8 inches on a side, by draping parchment paper so that two opposite sides can be used as grips.
2. In a bowl, melt the butter on high for one minute in the microwave. Add oats, flour, brown sugar, ginger, and salt to the mixture. Stir until completely blended, and clumps form. Reserve 1/2 cup of the crumble mixture, then press the remaining mixture into an equal layer on the bottom of the pan.
3. Spread the preserves over the crust evenly. Spread the saved oat mixture on top in a uniform layer.

4. Air-fry the bars for 35 to 40 minutes or until the topping has turned golden brown. Before slicing, place the pan on a wire rack to cool fully.

Per bar:

120 calories | 2 g protein | 13 g carbohydrates | 4 g fat (2.5 g sat fat) | 1 g fiber

FRENCH TOAST CUPS WITH RASPBERRIES

Serves 2 • Turnaround time: 15 minutes • Total time: 35 minutes + chilling time

Ingredients

- 2 slices of Italian bread (about 2 ounces), cut into ½-inch cubes, divided
- ½ cup fresh or frozen raspberries
- 2 ounces fat-free cream cheese, cut into ¼-inch cubes
- 2 large eggs
- ½ cup reduced-fat 2% milk
- 3 tablespoons light pancake syrup, divided
- ½ teaspoon vanilla extract

Method

1. Spray two eight-ounce custard cups with nonstick cooking spray.
2. Place a fourth of the bread cubes in the bottom of each custard cup. Sprinkle raspberries and cream cheese cubes on the toast. Add the remaining bread on top.
3. In a bowl, whisk the eggs, milk, 1 tablespoon of syrup, and vanilla. Pour the mixture over the bread. Refrigerate for at least one hour.

11

4. Preheat the air fryer to 325F. Place the custard cups in the basket of the air fryer. 12 to 15 minutes, or until golden brown and puffy.
5. Serve with the remaining 2 tablespoons of syrup poured over the top.

Per serving:

260 calories | 16 g protein | 33 g carbohydrates | 7 g fat (2.8 g sat fat) | 3 g fiber

APPLE DUTCH BABY PANCAKE

Serves 2 • Turnaround time: 10 minutes • Total time: 55 minutes

Ingredients

- ¼ cup all-purpose flour
- 4 tablespoons sugar, divided
- ¼ teaspoon baking powder
- ¼ teaspoon ground cinnamon
- Pinch of salt
- ½ cup reduced-fat 2% milk
- 2 large eggs
- ½ teaspoon vanilla extract
- 1 tablespoon unsalted butter
- 1 small apple, cored and thinly sliced
- 2 tablespoons light pancake syrup

Method

1. Mix the flour, 2 tablespoons of sugar, baking powder, cinnamon, and salt together well in a bowl.

2. In a separate dish, thoroughly combine the milk, eggs, and vanilla extract. Lightly whisk the milk mixture, then add the flour mixture slowly while constantly beating until fully incorporated. Allow the batter to rest for thirty minutes.
3. Preheat the air fryer to 400Fahrenheit.
4. Place the butter in a 6-inch round baking pan and air fry for one minute until the butter has melted and the pan is hot.
5. Brush a portion of the butter up the pan's sides, then sprinkle 1 tablespoon of sugar over the butter. Arrange the apple slices in a single layer in the baking dish. Sprinkle the apples with the remaining 1 tablespoon of sugar. Air-fry the mixture for 2 minutes or until it bubbles.
6. Pour the batter mixture over the apples with care. Reduce the air fryer temperature to 350 Fahrenheit and air fry the batter for 12 minutes, or until the sides are golden brown and the center is cooked through. Serve pancakes drizzled with pancake syrup.

Per serving:

320 calories | 8 g protein | 57 g carbohydrates | 7 g fat (4.4 g sat fat) | 2 g fiber

CHEESY BACON & EGG CUPS

Serves 4 • Turnaround time: 10 minutes • Total time: 22 minutes

Ingredients

- 4 large eggs
- Salt and freshly ground black pepper
- 2 ounces Canadian bacon, chopped
- ¼ red bell pepper, finely chopped
- ½ cup reduced-fat shredded Cheddar cheese, divided
- 1 tablespoon chopped fresh chives (optional)

Method

1. Preheat the air fryer to 400F. Coat four silicone muffin cups lightly with vegetable oil.
2. In a bowl, whisk the eggs and season with salt and pepper. Add the bacon, pepper, and a portion of the cheese. Combine the ingredients until they are fully blended. In a muffin tin, divide the egg mixture and top with the remaining cheese.

3. Air-fry for 12 to 15 minutes, or until thoroughly done. Garnish with fresh chives (if using).

Per serving

130 calories | 13 g protein | 1 g carbohydrates | 8 g fat (3.3 g sat fat) | 0 g fiber

SUNNY-SIDE-UP EGGS IN AVOCADO

Serves 2 • Turnaround time: 5 minutes • Total time: 14 minutes

Ingredients

- 1 Haas avocado, halved and pitted
- 2 large eggs
- Salt and freshly ground black pepper
- Chopped fresh parsley for garnish (optional)
- 1 lime, cut into wedges (optional)

Method

1. Preheat the air fryer to 400F.
2. Cut a thin slice off each avocado half's rounded bottom to keep it from rolling around in the air fryer basket.
3. Crack an egg immediately into each avocado half's hollow.
4. Air-fry for 9 minutes, pausing halfway through to determine if the egg whites are set and the yolk is cooked to the required degree.
5. Season with salt and pepper to taste, and top with chopped parsley (if using). Serve with slices of lime (if using).

Per serving

185 calories | 8 g protein | 6 g carbohydrates | 15 g fat (3 g sat fat) | 5 g fiber

ENGLISH MUFFIN BREAKFAST PIZZAS

Serves 2 • Turnaround time: 5 minutes • Total time: 15 minutes

Ingredients:

- 2 whole-grain English muffins, split
- 1 Roma tomato, thinly sliced
- Salt and freshly ground black pepper
- ½ cup shredded part-skim mozzarella cheese
- 2 vegetarian breakfast sausage patties, crumbled
- Pinch of dried oregano

Method

1. Preheat the air fryer to 400F.
2. Place the muffin halves, cut side up, in the basket of an air fryer. 3 minutes in the air fryer till heated.
3. Season the tomatoes with salt and pepper to taste. Place the tomato slices on top of the muffins, followed by an equal amount of cheese and sausage and a pinch of oregano.
4. Continue air-frying for a further 5 minutes, or until the cheese has melted and begun to color.

Per serving:

285 calories | 21 g protein | 32 g carbohydrates | 9 g fat (3.4 g sat fat) | 6 g fiber

BERRY CREAMY BREAKFAST SANDWICHES

Serves 4 • Turnaround time: 10 minutes • Total time: 15 minutes

Ingredients

- 4 ounces soft goat cheese
- 1 tablespoon honey
- 8 slices of whole wheat bread
- 1 cup blackberries

Method

1. Preheat the air fryer to 350F.
2. In a bowl, combine the goat cheese and honey with a fork to create a smooth spread. Spread the cheese mixture equally on each slice of bread, almost to the edges.
3. Spread the berries on four bread pieces and top with the remaining slices. Spray the sandwiches lightly with flavorless cooking oil, such as avocado oil.
4. Working in batches if required, position the sandwiches, so they are not touching in the air fryer basket. Toasted in an air fryer for five to seven minutes, or until toasted.

Per serving:

285 calories | 14 g protein | 35 g carbohydrates | 10 g fat (6.1 g sat fat) | 4 g fiber

CHILAQUILES

Serves 1 • Turnaround time: 5 minutes • Total time: 15 minutes

Ingredients

- 3 (6-inch) corn tortillas
- Pinch of kosher salt
- ½ cup green enchilada sauce
- 1 teaspoon unsalted butter
- 1 large egg
- ¼ red onion, thinly sliced
- 1 tablespoon crumbled Cotija cheese
- Hot sauce for serving (optional)

Method

1. Preheat the air fryer to 360F.
2. Spray oil on both sides of each tortilla and sprinkle with salt. Stack and cut the tortillas into six wedges. Spread the tortillas out in the air fryer basket to allow for air circulation. Air-fry for 5 minutes, shaking the basket halfway through until the chips begin to brown.

3. Transfer the chips to a bowl. Toss them with the enchilada sauce until they are evenly coated. Return the chips to the basket of the air fryer and air fry for an additional 3 minutes until lightly browned.
4. In the meantime, melt the butter over medium heat in a small skillet and cook the egg to your liking.
5. Add the egg, onion pieces, cheese, and a sprinkle of spicy sauce to the chips on a dish (if using).

Per serving

385 calories | 14 g protein | 39 g carbohydrates | 20 g fat (9.8 g sat fat) | 6 g fiber

Chapter 3: Lunch Recipes

PISTACHIO-CRUSTED CHICKEN WITH POMEGRANATE GLAZE

Serves 4 • Turnaround time: 10 minutes • Total time: 20 minutes

Ingredients

- 2 boneless, skinless chicken breasts (about 1½ pounds)
- Salt and freshly ground black pepper
- ¼ cup reduced-fat mayonnaise
- ½ cup chopped shelled pistachios
- 1 (5-ounce) bag baby arugula
- 2 tablespoons pomegranate or balsamic glaze for garnish

Method

1. Prepare the bottom of the air fryer basket by cutting a piece of parchment paper to size. Preheat the air fryer to 400F.
2. Using a long, sharp knife, slice each chicken breast horizontally, beginning on the thicker side until you reach the other side, to create four cutlets. Salt and pepper are used as seasonings. Both sides of the cutlets should be lightly coated in mayonnaise.

3. Place the pistachios in a shallow dish. Arrange the cutlets on the parchment paper so that they are not touching the air fryer basket. Air-fry for 8 to 10 minutes, or until brown and fully cooked.
4. Then rest the meat for five minutes before serving over arugula with the glaze drizzled on top.

Per serving

360 calories | 43 g protein | 8 g carbohydrates | 18 g fat (3 g sat fat) | 2 g fiber

CALIFORNIA-STYLE TURKEY BURGERS

Serves 4 • Turnaround time: 10 minutes • Total time: 25 minutes

- 1 pound 93% lean ground turkey
- 1 tablespoon Dijon mustard
- 1 tablespoon reduced-fat mayonnaise
- Salt and freshly ground black pepper
- 4 hamburger buns with sesame seeds
- 4 slices of low-fat Monterey Jack cheese
- ½ cup shredded carrot
- ½ cup baby spinach
- 1 tomato, thinly sliced

Method

1. Preheat the air fryer to 360F.
2. In a bowl, combine the turkey, Dijon mustard, and mayonnaise. Salt and pepper are used as seasonings. Mix until fully blended, then divide and form into four patties.
3. Arrange the patties so that they are not touching the air fryer basket. Air-fry burgers for 15 minutes, pausing halfway through cooking time to flip them.
4. Patties should be browned and 165F in the thickest part.

5. Before serving, place the burgers on the buns and top with cheese, carrots, spinach, and tomato slices.

Per serving

380 calories | 33 g protein | 22 g carbohydrates | 19 g fat (7 g sat fat) | 4 g fiber

THAI CHICKEN SKEWERS WITH PEANUT SAUCE

Serves 4 • Turnaround time: 15 minutes • Total time: 25 minutes + marinating time

Ingredients

Chicken skewers

- 2 tablespoons Thai red curry paste
- 2 tablespoons canola oil
- 1 tablespoon fresh lime juice
- 2 cloves garlic, minced
- 1½ pounds of chicken tenders

Peanut Sauce

- ⅓ cup creamy peanut butter
- Juice of ½ lime
- 1 tablespoon reduced-sodium soy sauce

28

- 1 teaspoon brown sugar
- 1 teaspoon grated fresh ginger
- 1 teaspoon chili-garlic sauce
- ¼ cup water

Method

1. To create the chicken skewers, combine the curry paste, oil, lime juice, and garlic in a small bowl until smooth. Place the mixture in a large resealable plastic bag.
2. Add the chicken, seal the bag, and massage the bag to uniformly coat the chicken. Marinate 1 hour (or up to 8 hours) in the refrigerator
3. To prepare the peanut sauce, combine the peanut butter, lime juice, soy sauce, brown sugar, ginger, and chili-garlic sauce in a bowl.
4. Add the water slowly and whisk until smooth. Refrigerate until ready to use, covered.
5. To complete the meal, heat the air fryer to 400F.
6. Discard the marinade and thread the chicken back and forth onto air fryer-compatible metal skewers. Using as many batches as necessary, air-fry the skewers for 10 minutes.
7. Halfway through the cooking period, flip the skewers and bast them lightly with a few teaspoons of peanut sauce.
8. Serve the remaining peanut sauce as a dipping sauce.
9. Covered and refrigerated, the peanut sauce can be stored for up to one week.

Per serving

410 calories | 45 g protein | 8 g carbohydrates | 23 g fat (4 g sat fat) | 1 g fiber

CHICKEN FAJITAS

Serves 4 • Turnaround time: 15 minutes • Total time: 30 minutes

- 1 pound chicken breast tenders, chopped into bite-size pieces
- ½ onion, thinly sliced
- ½ red bell pepper, seeded and thinly sliced
- ½ green bell pepper, seeded and thinly sliced
- 1 tablespoon vegetable oil
- 1 tablespoon fajita seasoning
- 1 teaspoon kosher salt
- Juice of ½ lime
- 8 small flour tortillas
- ½ cup guacamole

Method

1. Preheat the air fryer to 400F.
2. Combine the chicken, onion, and peppers in a bowl. Drizzle the vegetable oil over the vegetables and toss until evenly coated. Toss in the fajita seasoning and salt again.
3. Arrange the chicken and vegetables in a single layer in the air fryer basket, working in batches if required. 15 minutes of air-frying, halting halfway through.
4. Shake the basket during the cooking period until the vegetables are soft and the chicken is fully cooked.

5. Transfer the mixture to a dish and sprinkle it with fresh lime juice.
6. Serve the tortillas with guacamole and the chicken mixture.

Per serving:

410 calories | 32 g protein | 37 g carbohydrates | 15 g fat (3.1 g sat fat) | 5 g fiber

GENERAL TSO'S CHICKEN

Serves 4 • Turnaround time: 10 minutes • Total time: 25 minutes

Ingredients

- 4 boneless, skinless chicken thighs (about 1¼ pounds)
- Salt and freshly ground black pepper
- 2 tablespoons cornstarch
- 2 tablespoons rice vinegar
- 2 tablespoons reduced-sodium soy sauce
- 2 teaspoons hoisin sauce
- 2 tablespoons sugar
- 2 cloves garlic, minced
- 1 teaspoon sriracha (optional)
- 2 scallions, thinly sliced
- 1 tablespoon sesame seeds

Ingredients

1. Preheat the air fryer to 400F.
2. Cut the chicken into small pieces and arrange them in a big bowl. Salt and pepper are used as seasonings. Coat the vegetables with cornstarch and mix.

3. Spread the chicken in a single layer in the air fryer basket and mist lightly with olive oil. Air-fry for 15 minutes, shaking the food midway through cooking.
4. Whisk together the vinegar, soy sauce, hoisin sauce, sugar, garlic, and sriracha in a separate bowl. Place the chicken in a bowl and mix well to coat
5. Before serving, garnish with scallions and sesame seeds.

Per serving:

270 calories | 28 g protein | 17 g carbohydrates | 10 g fat (2.9 g sat fat) | 1 g fiber

CHINESE CHICKEN PATTIES

Serves 4 • Turnaround time: 10 minutes • Total time: 20 minutes

Ingredients

- 1½ pounds extra-lean ground chicken breast
- 1 (8-ounce) can (drained and chopped)water chestnuts
- 3 tablespoons hoisin sauce
- 3 scallions, thinly sliced
- 1 tablespoon grated fresh ginger

Method

1. Preheat the air fryer to 400F.
2. In a bowl, thoroughly incorporate the chicken, water chestnuts, hoisin sauce, scallions, and ginger. Form eight patties, each about half an inch thick.
3. Place the patties in the air fryer basket in a single layer. Lightly mist with olive oil. Air-fry for 10 minutes or until the thickest area of the patty reaches 165 F.

Per serving:

240 calories | 36 g protein | 12 g carbohydrates | 6 g fat (1 g sat fat) | 2 g fiber

CHICKEN COBB SALAD WITH BUFFALO DRIZZLE

Serves 4 • Turnaround time: 20 minutes • Total time: 35 minutes

Ingredients

- 2 boneless (about 1 pound) skinless chicken breasts
- Salt and freshly ground black pepper
- 2 tablespoons unsalted butter
- 2 tablespoons hot sauce
- 2 tablespoons olive oil
- 2 teaspoons cider vinegar
- 8 cups chopped romaine
- 2 hard-boiled eggs, chopped
- ¼ cup crumbled blue cheese
- 1 cup cherry tomatoes, chopped
- ¼ cup chopped red onion
- 1 avocado, halved, pitted, and chopped

Method

1. Preheat the air fryer to 380F.

2. Season the chicken with salt and pepper. Lightly spritz with olive oil spray. Place the chicken in the air fryer basket in a single layer. Air-fry the chicken for 15 to 20 minutes, pausing halfway during the cooking time to flip it.
3. In the meantime, heat the butter in a bowl on high for one minute. Reserve.
4. In another large dish, thoroughly blend the olive oil and vinegar using a whisk. Season with salt and pepper to taste. Add the romaine lettuce and toss to coat.
5. Arrange the avocado, eggs, blue cheese, tomatoes, and red onion on top.
6. When the chicken is cool enough to handle, slice it into thin strips or chop it into bite-sized pieces, then add it to the butter mixture. Toss until the chicken is completely coated. Top the salad with the chicken and drizzle with any remaining sauce.

Per serving:

395 calories | 33 g protein | 7 g carbohydrates | 26 g fat (8.2 g sat fat) | 4 g fiber

HAWAIIAN PORK CHOPS WITH PINEAPPLE

Serves 4 • Turnaround time: 10 minutes • Total time: 20 minutes + marinating time

Ingredients

- 3 tablespoons Worcestershire sauce
- 1 tablespoon brown sugar
- 1 tablespoon grated fresh ginger
- ½ teaspoon red pepper flakes (optional)
- 4 center-cut boneless pork chops (about 1½ pounds)
- 4 slices of fresh pineapple, each about ½ inch thick
- 2 scallions, thinly sliced

Method

1. In a shallow bowl, thoroughly combine Worcestershire sauce, brown sugar, ginger, and red pepper flakes. After turning the pork to coat, marinate it at room temperature for 30 minutes while turning it once.
2. Preheat the air fryer to 400F.
3. Arrange the pork in the basket of the air fryer so that the pieces do not touch, and lightly spray with olive oil. Air-fry for 10 minutes, halting the cooking process halfway through.

37

4. Turn the chops and place a pineapple ring on top of each chop until the chops are browned, and a meat thermometer inserted into the thickest piece registers 145F.
5. Allow it to rest for 5 minutes before serving with scallions.

Per serving:

325 calories | 38 g protein | 13 g carbohydrates | 13 g fat (4.6 g sat fat) | 1 g fiber

EASY WEEKNIGHT PORK KEBABS

Serves 4 • Turnaround time: 15 minutes • Total time: 25 minutes

Ingredients

- ¼ cup orange juice
- 2 tablespoons honey
- 2 tablespoons Worcestershire sauce
- 1 tablespoon olive oil
- 1 large clove of garlic, minced
- 2 bell peppers, preferably red or orange
- 1 pork tenderloin (about 1¼ pounds)

Method

1. In a bowl, whisk the orange juice, honey, Worcestershire sauce, olive oil, and garlic.
2. Remove the peppers' tops, scrape out the seeds, then chop each pepper into eight equal pieces. Cut the pork into sixteen equal pieces. Transfer the peppers and pork to the bowl containing the marinade and stir until well coated.
3. Preheat the air fryer to 400F.

4. Thread the pork and peppers onto four metal skewers that will fit within the air fryer basket. Arrange the kebabs in the air fryer basket so they are not touching and air can circulate around them.
5. Fry the kebabs for 10 to 12 minutes, pausing halfway through cooking time to flip them.

Per serving:

250 calories | 31 g protein | 16 g carbohydrates | 7 g fat (1.5 g sat fat) | 1 g fiber

FAVORITE LEMON CHICKEN

Serves 4 • Turnaround time: 10 minutes • Total time: 30 minutes

Ingredients

- 4 boneless, skinless chicken breasts (about 1½ pounds)
- 1 tablespoon olive oil
- 1½ teaspoons lemon-pepper seasoning
- ½ teaspoon paprika
- ½ teaspoon garlic powder
- ¼ teaspoon dried oregano
- ¼ teaspoon freshly ground black pepper
- Juice of ½ lemon

Method

1. Preheat the air fryer to 360F.
2. Place the chicken in a bowl, sprinkle with olive oil, and season with salt and pepper. Add the lemon-pepper seasoning, paprika, garlic powder, oregano, and pepper to the top of the dish. Toss until everything is evenly coated.

3. Place the chicken in a single layer in the air fryer basket, working in batches if required. Air-fry the chicken for 20 to 25 minutes, pausing halfway during the cooking time to flip the pieces.
4. Transfer the chicken to a serving tray and drizzle it with lemon juice.

Per serving:

225 calories | 39 g protein | 0 g carbohydrates | 7 g fat (1.7 g sat fat) | 0 g fiber

SIMPLY TERRIFIC TURKEY MEATBALLS

Serves 4 • Turnaround time: 10 minutes • Total time: 20 minutes

Ingredients

- ¼ sweet onion
- 2 cloves garlic, coarsely chopped
- ¼ cup coarsely chopped fresh parsley
- 1 pound 8.5% lean ground turkey
- 1 large egg, lightly beaten
- ¾ cup panko breadcrumbs
- 1 teaspoon salt
- ½ teaspoon freshly ground black pepper

Method

1. Preheat the air fryer to 400F.
2. Finely chop the onion, garlic, and parsley. The vegetables should be placed in a bowl.

3. Add the ground turkey, egg, breadcrumbs, salt, and pepper to the pan. Blend with vigor until well combined. Form the mixture into meatballs measuring 1 1/4 inches in diameter.
4. Arrange the meatballs in a single layer in the air fryer basket, working in batches if required; spray liberally with olive oil. Air-fry for 7 to 10 minutes, pausing halfway through.
5. Shake the basket halfway through the cooking period until the meatballs are gently browned.

Per serving:

300 calories | 23 g protein | 16 g carbohydrates | 14 g fat (3.5 g sat fat) | 0 g fiber

ROAST BEEF WITH HORSERADISH CREAM

Serves 6 • Turnaround time: 10 minutes • Total time: 45 minutes

Ingredients

Roasted Beef

- 2 pounds beef roast top round or eye of round
- 1 tablespoon salt
- 2 teaspoons garlic powder
- 1 teaspoon freshly ground black pepper
- 1 teaspoon dried thyme

Horseradish Cream

- ⅓ cup fat-free half-and-half
- ⅓ cup reduced-fat sour cream
- ⅓ cup prepared horseradish
- 2 teaspoons fresh lemon juice
- Salt and freshly ground black pepper

Method

1. Preheat the air fryer to 400F.
2. To Prepare the roast beef, you must season the beef with salt, garlic powder, black pepper, and thyme. Place the beef fat-side down in the basket of an air fryer and spray lightly with olive oil. Air-fry the beef for 35 to 45 minutes. Flip once.
3. Temperatures range from 125°F (rare) to 150°F (medium). Ten minutes of rest is required before slicing the steak.
4. To make horseradish cream, you must thoroughly blend half-and-half sour cream, horseradish, and lemon juice with a whisk. Season with salt and pepper to taste. Serve.

Per serving:

235 calories | 35 g protein | 4 g carbohydrates | 8 g fat (3.3 g sat fat) | 0 g fiber

Chapter 4: Dinner Recipes

PORK TENDERLOIN WITH APRICOT GLAZE

Serves 4 • Turnaround time: 10 minutes • Total time: 28 minutes

Ingredients

- ⅓ cup apricot preserves
- 1 tablespoon Dijon mustard
- 1 pork tenderloin (about 1 pound)
- 2 teaspoons olive oil
- ½ teaspoon dried thyme
- ½ teaspoon salt
- ¼ teaspoon black pepper

Method

1. Preheat the air fryer to 360F.
2. In a bowl, thoroughly blend the preserves and Dijon mustard using a whisk. Set aside.
3. Rub olive oil, thyme, salt, and pepper into the meat. Arrange the pork in the basket of an air fryer. Air-fry the pork for 18 to 20 minutes, pausing midway through cooking time to turn the pig and brush with half the glaze.
4. Two to three minutes before the meat is finished cooking, re-glaze-it. Wait five minutes before chopping the meat.

Per serving:

205 calories | 24 g protein | 16 g carbohydrates | 5 g fat (1.1 g sat fat) | 0 g fiber

CUBAN TENDERLOIN

Serves 4 • Turnaround time: 10 minutes • Total time: 30 minutes + marinating time

Ingredients

- 1 pork tenderloin (about 1 pound)
- ½ cup orange juice
- Juice of 1 lime
- 1 tablespoon olive oil
- 2 teaspoons ground cumin
- 6 cloves garlic, chopped
- ½ teaspoon salt
- ¼ teaspoon freshly ground black pepper
- ¼ cup chopped fresh cilantro

Method

1. Combine the pork, orange juice, lime juice, olive oil, cumin, garlic, salt, and pepper in a large resealable bag. Massage the pork lightly to coat it. Marinate it for at least four hours or overnight.
2. Preheat the air fryer to 360F. Take the pork out of the marinade and dispose of the marinade.
3. Place the pork in the basket of an air fryer and spray lightly with olive oil. Air-fry the pork for 18 to 20 minutes, pausing halfway through cooking time to flip it.
4. Allow the pork to rest for 5 before slicing. Serve with some cilantro on top.

Per serving:

140 calories | 24 g protein | 2 g carbohydrates | 4 g fat (1 g sat fat) | 0 g fiber

GARLIC ROSEMARY PORK CHOPS WITH ROASTED ASPARAGUS

Serves 2 • Turnaround time: 10 minutes • Total time: 20 minutes

Ingredients

- 8 ounces asparagus spears
- Salt and freshly ground black pepper
- 2 bone-in pork chops (about 12 ounces)
- 1 teaspoon olive oil
- 2 cloves garlic, minced
- 1 teaspoon Italian seasoning
- 2 tablespoons pesto
- 2 rosemary sprigs for garnish

Method

1. Preheat the air fryer to 380F.
2. Remove the ends of the asparagus spears. Lightly mist with olive oil and season with salt and pepper to taste. Set aside.

3. The pork chops are drizzled with olive oil and then seasoned with garlic, Italian seasoning, salt, and pepper. The pork chops should be well covered with the glaze.
4. After seasoning the pork chops, place them in the air fryer basket, so they are not touching.
5. Cook for 10 to 12 minutes, flipping the pork chops halfway through and adding the asparagus or untilt the chops reaches 145F.
6. Let it rest for 5 minutes.
7. Top with pesto and rosemary, and serve.

Per serving:

250 calories | 25 g protein | 6 g carbohydrates | 15 g fat (3.3 g sat fat) | 2 g fiber

HAM AND CHEESE CALZONES

Serves 4 • Turnaround time: 10 minutes • Total time: 20 minutes

Ingredients

- 2 tablespoons all-purpose flour
- 12 ounces pizza dough, divided into 4 equal pieces
- 8 ounces deli ham
- 1 cup shredded part-skim mozzarella cheese
- ¼ cup finely chopped red onion
- 2 teaspoons olive oil, divided
- 1 cup marinara sauce

Method

1. Preheat the air fryer to 360F.
2. Dust your workspace lightly with flour, and then roll out each piece of pizza dough into a thin circle. Spread ham, cheese, and red onion on one half of each dough circle. The other side is folded over the top to produce a half-circle. Pull the edges together. Lightly brush each calzone with 1/2 tsp of olive oil.
3. If required, place the calzones in the air fryer basket in batches. Air-fry for 10 minutes, or until browned gently.

4. In the meantime, cook the marinara sauce for one minute on high in a microwave-safe bowl. Serve with the calzones.

Per serving:

425 calories | 24 g protein | 49 g carbohydrates | 14 g fat (4.8 g sat fat) | 3 g fiber

KOREAN BEEF IN LETTUCE CUPS

Serves 4 • Turnaround time: 20 minutes • Total time: 30 minutes + marinating time

Ingredients

- 2 tablespoons gochujang (Korean chile paste)
- 2 cloves garlic, minced
- 2 teaspoons grated fresh ginger
- 1 tablespoon toasted sesame oil
- 1 tablespoon reduced-sodium soy sauce
- 1 tablespoon sesame seeds
- 2 teaspoons sugar
- ½ teaspoon salt
- 1 pound thinly sliced sirloin, trimmed of visible fat
- 1 small red onion, thinly sliced
- 2 heads of butter lettuce, leaves separated into "cups."
- 4 scallions, thinly sliced
- 1 cup kimchi

Method

1. Combine the gochujang, garlic, ginger, sesame oil, soy sauce, sesame seeds, sugar, and salt in a bowl. Place the meat and onions along with the marinade in a resealable bag and massage until evenly coated. Marinate thirty minutes at room temperature or up to 24 hours in the refrigerator.
2. Preheat the air fryer to 400F.
3. Transfer the meat and onions to the basket of an air fryer, reserving as much of the marinade as possible and arranging the meat in an equal layer. Throw out the marinade. Air-fry for 10 minutes, pausing halfway through to flip the meat until browned and thoroughly done.
4. To serve, split the beef and onions amongst the cups of lettuce and top with the scallions and kimchi.

Per serving:

280 calories | 29 g protein | 8 g carbohydrates | 14 g fat (4.6 g sat fat) | 3 g fiber

HOMESTYLE MEATLOAF

Serves 4 • Turnaround time: 15 minutes • Total time: 1 hour

Ingredients

- 1 small onion, coarsely chopped
- 1 rib celery, coarsely chopped
- 2 cloves garlic
- 1 pound 85% lean ground beef
- 1 large egg, lightly beaten
- ½ cup panko breadcrumbs
- 2 tablespoons milk
- 1 teaspoon salt
- ½ teaspoon freshly ground black pepper
- 2 tablespoons ketchup
- 1 tablespoon brown sugar

Method

1. Preheat the air fryer to 350F. Coat a circular 8-inch baking dish with olive oil and set aside.
2. In a food processor fitted with a metal blade, finely chop the onion, celery, and garlic. The vegetables should be placed in a bowl.

3. Add the beef, egg, breadcrumbs, milk, salt, and pepper to the pan. Blend vigorously until well combined. Transfer the mixture to the loaf pan and form it into a loaf shape.
4. Mix the ketchup and brown sugar in a bowl. Spread the glaze evenly over the meatloaf using the back of a spoon.
5. Air-fry the meatloaf for 45 minutes, or until the meat reaches 160F. Remove the food from the air fryer and allow it to rest for approximately 10 minutes before slicing.

Per serving:

295 calories | 22 g protein | 18 g carbohydrates | 13 g fat (5 g sat fat) | 0 g fiber

SPICY ROASTED SHRIMP

Serves 4 • Turnaround time: 5 minutes • Total time: 20 minutes

Ingredients

- 2 tablespoons olive oil
- 3 cloves garlic, minced
- Juice of 1 lemon
- 1 teaspoon salt
- ½ teaspoon freshly ground black pepper
- ½ teaspoon paprika
- ¼ teaspoon red pepper flakes (optional)
- 1½ pounds (peeled and deveined) large uncooked shrimp
- 2 tablespoons chopped fresh cilantro

Method

1. Preheat the air fryer to 370F.

2. Combine the olive oil, garlic, lemon juice, salt, pepper, paprika, and red pepper flakes in a large bowl. Add the shrimp and toss until coated evenly.
3. Transfer the shrimp to the basket of an air fryer. Air-fry, the shrimp for 12 to 15 minutes, pausing halfway through to shake the basket until fully done.
4. Before serving, garnish the dish with cilantro.

Per serving:

185 calories | 23 g protein | 3 g carbohydrates | 9 g fat (1.4 g sat fat) | 0 g fiber

BETTER-THAN-TAKEOUT SHRIMP AND BROCCOLI

Serves 4 • Turnaround time: 10 minutes • Total time: 25 minutes

Ingredients

- 2 tablespoons reduced-sodium soy sauce
- 1 tablespoon sesame oil
- 2 teaspoons chile-garlic sauce
- 3 cloves garlic, minced
- 1 teaspoon grated fresh ginger
- 1½ pounds (peeled and deveined) large uncooked shrimp
- 4 cups broccoli florets
- ¼ cup sesame seeds

Method

1. Preheat the air fryer to 370F.
2. Combine the soy sauce, sesame oil, chile-garlic sauce, garlic, and ginger in a bowl. Add the shrimp and broccoli to the pan and mix until evenly covered.

3. Transfer the shrimp and broccoli to the basket of an air fryer. Air-fry the shrimp for 12 to 15 minutes (pausing halfway through cooking to shake the basket) or until fully cooked and the broccoli is soft.
4. Before serving, sprinkle sesame seeds on top of the dish.

Per serving:

245 calories | 28 g protein | 9 g carbohydrates | 11 g fat (1.8 g sat fat) | 4 g fiber

BARBECUE-GLAZED SALMON

Serves 4 • Turnaround time: 10 minutes • Total time: 18 minutes

Ingredients

- ½ cup barbecue sauce
- 2 tablespoons honey
- 1¼ pounds salmon fillets
- ½ teaspoon salt
- 2 scallions, thinly sliced

Method

1. Cut a piece of paper to fit the basket's bottom and set it aside. Preheat the air fryer to 400F.
2. Whisk together the barbecue sauce and honey in a bowl.
3. Sprinkle salt on the fish and coat it lightly with the sauce. Arrange the fish skin-side down on the parchment, leaving space between each piece.
4. Air-fry the fish for 5 minutes, pausing halfway through to bast it with the remaining sauce. Continue air-frying for an additional 3 to 5 minutes, or until the fish flakes easily with a fork.
5. Allow it to rest for 5 minutes before serving. Garnish with onions if desired.

Per serving:

365 calories | 29 g protein | 25 g carbohydrates | 16 g fat (3.2 g sat fat) | 0 g fiber

MISO-GLAZED COD

Serves 4 • Turnaround time: 10 minutes • Total time: 18 minutes

Ingredients

- 1 tablespoon unsalted butter, melted
- ¼ cup white miso paste
- 2 tablespoons honey
- 1 tablespoon rice wine vinegar
- ½ teaspoon grated fresh ginger
- 1½ pounds cod
- Salt and freshly ground black pepper
- 1 teaspoon toasted sesame oil

Method

1. Cut a piece of paper to fit the basket's bottom and set it aside. Preheat the air fryer to 400F.
2. In a small bowl, whisk together the butter, miso, honey, vinegar, and ginger in a small bowl until smooth.

3. Season the fish with salt and pepper, followed by a light coating of oil and half of the sauce. Arrange the fish on the parchment with space between the parts.
4. Air-fry the fish for 5 minutes, pausing halfway through to bast it with the remaining sauce. Continue air-frying for an additional 3 to 5 minutes, or until the fish is fully done. It easily flaked with a fork.

Per serving:

250 calories | 32 g protein | 15 g carbohydrates | 6 g fat (2.4 g sat fat) | 1 g fiber

LEMON-PEPPER TILAPIA

Serves 4 • Turnaround time: 10 minutes • Total time: 18 minutes

Ingredients

- 1½ pounds tilapia
- 2 teaspoons olive oil
- 2 teaspoons lemon-pepper seasoning
- 1 teaspoon paprika (optional)
- 4 lemon slices

Method

1. Cut a piece of paper to fit the basket's bottom and set it aside. Preheat the air fryer to 400F.
2. Lightly coat the tilapia with oil and season both sides with lemon-pepper spice and paprika (if using). Place the fish on the parchment with space between each piece.
3. Cook the fish in an air fryer for 8 minutes or until it flakes easily with a fork. Serve with lemon slices.

Per serving:

185 calories | 33 g protein | 0 g carbohydrates | 6 g fat (1.5 g sat fat) | 0 g fiber

VEGETARIAN SHEPHERD'S PIE

Serves 4 • Turnaround time: 10 minutes • Total time: 40 minutes

Ingredients

- 2 teaspoons olive oil
- 1 small onion, chopped
- 1 small carrot, chopped
- Salt and freshly ground black pepper
- 1 (10-ounce) package of frozen plant-based meat crumbles
- ½ cup crushed tomatoes
- ½ teaspoon dried thyme
- 1 cup frozen peas
- 2 cups mashed potatoes
- ½ cup reduced-fat Cheddar cheese

Method

1. Place the baking dish in the air fryer basket and set the temperature to 350 F. Air-fry the onion for 5 minutes or until it begins to soften.
2. Carefully add the beef crumbles and air fry for 5 minutes, or until the crumbles start to crackle. Add the tomatoes and thyme, and stir to mix completely.

3. On top of the vegetable combination, scatter the peas and sprinkle the mashed potatoes.
4. Air-fry for 15 minutes until thoroughly cooked. Spread the cheese on top and continue air-frying for 5 minutes until melted.

Per serving:

330 calories | 25 g protein | 28 g carbohydrates | 10 g fat (3 g sat fat) | 5 g fib

SWORDFISH STEAKS WITH CUCUMBER SALSA

Serves 2 • Turnaround time: 20 minutes • Total time: 30 minutes

Ingredients

Swordfish

- 2 teaspoons honey
- 2 teaspoons reduced-sodium soy sauce
- 2 swordfish steaks (about 12 ounces)

Cucumber Salsa

- 1 cucumber, peeled, seeded, and chopped
- ½ jalapeño pepper, seeded and finely chopped
- 1 scallion, thinly sliced
- Juice of ½ lime
- 2 tablespoons chopped fresh mint or cilantro
- Salt and freshly ground black pepper

Method

1. To prepare the swordfish, combine the honey and soy sauce in a shallow dish until smooth. Add the swordfish, turn to coat, and marinate for 15 minutes at room temperature, turning once. While marinating, preheat the air fryer to 400F.
2. In a bowl, combine the cucumber, jalapeno, scallion, lime juice, and mint or cilantro for the cucumber salsa. Season with salt and pepper to taste.
3. Place the fish in the basket of an air fryer and spray it with olive oil. Air-fry the fish for 10 minutes, pausing midway during the cooking time to flip the fish until it flakes easily with a fork.
4. The swordfish should be served with salsa.

Per serving:

265 calories | 31 g protein | 10 g carbohydrates | 10 g fat (2.5 g sat fat) | 1 g fiber

Chapter 5: Dessert Recipes

CINNAMON APPLE CHIPS

Serves 4 • Turnaround time: 5 minutes • Cook time: 20-25 minutes

Ingredients

- 2 tablespoons unsalted butter, melted
- 1 tablespoon brown sugar
- ½ teaspoon ground cinnamon
- Pinch of salt
- 2 large apples, cored

Method

1. Combine the brown sugar, butter, cinnamon, and salt in a bowl.
2. Slice the apples as thinly as possible into thin disks.
3. Toss the apple slices in the butter mixture until they are completely coated.
4. Place the apple slices in the air fryer basket without overlapping them. Adjust the temperature to 360F and air fry the chips in batches for 20 to 25 minutes, pausing once or twice to shake the basket and turn the chips.
5. As the chips cool, they will become crispier. Store it in a container with a lid at room temperature.

Per serving:

140 calories | 0 g protein | 21 g carbohydrates | 6 g fat (4 g sat fat) | 2.5 g fiber

ALMOND COOKIES

Serves 18 • Turnaround time: 10 minutes • Total time: 35 minutes

Ingredients

- 2 cups almonds
- 1 cup sugar
- 2 large egg whites
- ½ teaspoon almond extract

Method

1. Line the air fryer basket with parchment and preheat the air fryer to 300F.
2. In a food processor, grind the almonds until they resemble a fine meal. Add the sugar and continue blending for 15 seconds. Add the egg whites and almond extract, and continue blending for an additional 15 seconds, or until a smooth dough forms around the blade.
3. Using a teaspoon, divide the dough into 18 sections of equal size. Working in batches, space the cookies at least 1 1/2 inches apart in the air fryer. Air frying for 25 to 30 minutes, paused halfway through baking time to softly flatten the cookies with the back of a spoon.

Per cookie:

135 calories | 4 g protein | 15 g carbohydrates | 8 g fat (0.6 g sat fat) | 2 g fiber

PEANUT BUTTER CHOCOLATE CHIP COOKIES

Serves 16 • Turnaround time: 5 minutes • Total time: 10 minutes

Ingredients

- 1 cup creamy peanut butter
- 1 cup packed brown sugar
- 1 large egg
- ½ teaspoon vanilla extract
- ½ cup semisweet mini chocolate chips

Method

1. Preheat the air fryer to 350F. Spray the air fryer basket lightly with a flavorless oil, such as avocado.
2. Combine the peanut butter, brown sugar, egg, and vanilla in a large basin. Using a mixer, fully incorporate all the ingredients. Stir in the chocolate chips, then divide the dough into 16 halves of a similar size.
3. Make balls with the dough and flatten them with the back of a spoon.
4. Working in batches, if required, position the cookies so that they are not touching in the air fryer basket. Air-fry for 5 minutes until the food is browned. Allow it to cool in the basket for five minutes before transferring it to a cooling rack.

Per cookie:

180 calories | 4 g protein | 21 g carbohydrates | 10 g fat (2.7 g sat fat) | 1 g fiber

CHOCOLATE LAVA CAKE FOR TWO

Serves 2 • Turnaround time: 10 minutes • Total time: 20 minutes

Ingredients

- ¼ cup semisweet chocolate chips (about 1½ ounces)
- 2 tablespoons unsalted butter
- ¼ cup powdered sugar
- 1 large egg
- ¼ teaspoon vanilla extract
- Pinch of salt
- 1 tablespoon all-purpose flour
- ½ cup fresh raspberries

Method

1. Preheat the air fryer to 370F. Spray an 8-ounce ramekin lightly with a flavorless oil, such as avocado.
2. In a bowl, combine the chocolate chips and butter. Melt the butter and begin to melt the chocolate chips in the microwave on high for one minute. Blend until completely smooth.

75

3. Blend together the powdered sugar, egg, vanilla extract, and salt. Add the flour and whisk until it is completely combined. The chocolate mixture is transferred to the ready-to-use ramekin.
4. Place the ramekin in the basket of the air fryer. Air-fry for 8 to 10 minutes, or until the surface seems dry and slightly puffed. Let it rest for about 1 minute.
5. Loosen the sides with a butter knife and invert the cake onto a plate. Raspberries may be used as a garnish.

Per serving:

335 calories | 5 g protein | 36 g carbohydrates | 21 g fat (12 g sat fat) | 3 g fiber

CHEESECAKE BITES

Serves 15 • Turnaround time: 10 minutes • Total time: 20 minutes + chilling time

Ingredients

- 1 (1.9-ounce) package of mini phyllo pastry shells
- 1 (4-ounce) package Neufchâtel
- ¼ cup sugar
- 1 tablespoon fresh lemon zest
- ½ cup fat-free nondairy whipped topping
- 15 fresh raspberries

Method

1. Preheat the air fryer to 350F.
2. Working in batches, if necessary, arrange the pastry shells in the air fryer basket and spritz lightly with a neutral-flavored oil, such as avocado oil. Air fry for 5 to 7 minutes until golden. Transfer to a baking sheet and let cool completely before filling.
3. Meanwhile, using a mixer, beat the Neufchâtel, sugar, and lemon zest until smooth. Use a spatula to fold the whipped topping into the cheese mixture until thoroughly combined.

4. Fill each shell with about a scant tablespoon of the cheese mixture and top with a raspberry. Cover and refrigerate for 2 hours before serving.

Per serving:

50 calories | 1 g protein | 7 g carbohydrates | 2 g fat (1 g sat fat) | 0 g fiber

STRAWBERRY SHORTCAKE

Serves 4 • Turnaround time: 20 minutes • Total time: 32 minutes

Ingredients

- 2 cups sliced strawberries (about 1 pint)
- 1 tablespoon honey
- ¾ cup all-purpose flour, plus more for dusting
- 2 tablespoons sugar
- ¾ teaspoon baking powder
- ¼ teaspoon salt
- 2 tablespoons unsalted butter
- ⅓ cup low-fat buttermilk
- 1 large egg, lightly beaten
- ½ teaspoon vanilla extract
- 1 cup fat-free nondairy whipped topping

Method

1. In a bowl, combine the honey and strawberries. Stir the strawberries until they are evenly coated. Set aside.

2. Preheat the air fryer to 400F.
3. In a second large bowl, combine the flour, sugar, baking powder, and salt. With your fingertips, incorporate the butter into the flour mixture until it resembles a coarse meal.
4. In a bowl, whisk the egg, buttermilk, and vanilla. Stir into the flour mixture until a dough forms.
5. Turn out the dough onto a lightly floured work surface and divide it into four equal halves. Form each piece into a half-inch thick biscuit.
6. Arrange the biscuits so that they are not touching the air fryer basket. 12 to 15 minutes in the air fryer until golden. When the biscuits are cold enough to handle, divide them into halves.
7. Before serving, divide the strawberries and any remaining juices among the biscuits and top with whipped topping.

Per serving:

290 calories | 7 g protein | 48 g carbohydrates | 9 g fat (4.9 g sat fat) | 4 g fiber

CHERRY HAND PIES

Serves 8 • Turnaround time: 20 minutes • Total time: 30 minutes

Ingredients

- 1 (14-ounce) package refrigerated pie crust
- ½ cup all-fruit cherry preserves
- 1 large egg, lightly beaten
- 2 tablespoons sugar

Method

- Preheat the air fryer to 350F.
- The pie crusts should be rolled out on a lightly floured board. Cut each square crust into four smaller squares for a total of eight squares (discard the edges).
- In the center of each square, place one tablespoon of preserves. Fold one corner of the dough over and push it into the opposite corner to create a triangle.
- Create a triangle. Use a fork to create a crimped edge. Cut a small hole in the top with the tip of a knife to allow steam to escape. Coat the pies with an egg and then sprinkle with sugar.

- Arrange the pies in the air fryer basket so that they are not touching, working in batches if required. Air-fry for eight to ten minutes until golden brown. Serve it at room temperature or heated.

Per serving:

300 calories | 3 g protein | 30 g carbohydrates | 15 g fat (5.7 g sat fat) | 1 g fiber

BAKED APPLES

Serves 4 • Turnaround time: 10 minutes • Total time: 25 minutes

Ingredients

- 2 Honeycrisp apples
- ¼ cup chopped pecans
- 2 tablespoons brown sugar
- 1 tablespoon unsalted butter, softened
- 1 tablespoon golden raisins
- Pinch of ground cinnamon
- Pinch of salt

Method

1. Preheat the air fryer to 350F.
2. Halve the apples and remove the core and a portion of the flesh with a melon baller (leave the skin on).
3. Mix the nuts, brown sugar, butter, raisins, cinnamon, and salt in a small bowl. Fill the apple cavities with the nut mixture, gently pressing to ensure that the filling maintains its shape.

4. Pour half a cup of water into the air fryer basket's base to fill the drip pan. Place the apples in the basket of an air fryer. Air-fry apples for 15 minutes, or until tender and the tops begin to brown.

Per serving:

165 calories | 1 g protein | 24 g carbohydrates | 8 g fat (2.2 g sat fat) | 4 g fiber

BLUEBERRY CRISP

Serves 6 • Turnaround time: 10 minutes • Total time: 50 minutes

Ingredients

- 1 cup rolled oats
- ¼ cup all-purpose flour
- ¼ cup packed brown sugar
- ¼ teaspoon salt
- 3 tablespoons unsalted butter, melted
- 4 cups fresh blueberries
- ¼ cup granulated sugar
- 1 tablespoon cornstarch
- 1 tablespoon fresh lemon juice
- ¼ teaspoon ground nutmeg
- 6 small scoops of no-sugar vanilla ice cream (optional)

Method

1. Preheat the air fryer to 350F. Spray a 7-cup air fryer-compatible baking dish lightly with cooking spray. Set aside.

85

2. In a bowl, thoroughly blend the oats, flour, brown sugar, and salt with a whisk. With a fork, incorporate the butter until clumps begin to form. Set aside

3. Place the blueberries in the baking dish. Sprinkle the granulated sugar, cornstarch, lemon juice, and nutmeg over the blueberries. Stir until the blueberries are evenly coated. Spread into an equal layer, then sprinkle the oat mixture on top.

4. Air-fry for forty minutes, or until the top is golden brown and the berries are bubbling. Allow it to cool slightly before serving with ice cream (if using).

Per serving:

250 calories | 3 g protein | 46 g carbohydrates | 7 g fat (3.8 g sat fat) | 4 g fiber

ALMOND-STUFFED PEACHES

Serves 4 • Turnaround time: 15 minutes • Total time: 45 minutes

Ingredients

- 2 large peaches
- ½ cup finely chopped almonds
- 1 large egg white
- ¼ cup packed brown sugar
- ¼ teaspoon almond extract
- Pinch of ground cinnamon

Method

1. Preheat the air fryer to 350F.
2. Peach halves should be halved and the pits removed (do not peel). Arrange them cut-side up in an air fryer-compatible shallow baking dish.
3. Almonds, egg white, brown sugar, almond extract, and cinnamon should be completely blended in a small bowl.
4. Fill the cavities of each peach half with the almond mixture, gently pressing to ensure the shape is maintained. Lightly mist with neutral-flavored cooking oil, such as olive oil.
5. Wrap them in foil.
6. Air-fry the peaches for 25 minutes or until they are soft. Continue air-frying for a further 5 minutes or until the tops are golden.

Per serving:

205 calories | 6 g protein | 28 g carbohydrates | 9 g fat (0.7 g sat fat) | 4 g fiber

CONCLUSION

After reading this cookbook and trying out some of the recipes, you should have a good understanding of the many ways in which your air fryer can be put to good use. It doesn't matter how experienced a cook you are. The recipes in the Air Fryer Cookbook can be used by anyone. This book covers the basics as well as advanced techniques for using these new, trendy kitchen gadgets. The Air Fryer Cookbook has shown you how to make a tasty meal with no effort and taught you all the tricks of the trade. At present, the Air Fryer is the object of widespread interest, and for a good reason. To summarize, it improves the healthfulness, convenience, and tidiness of the cooking process. You can have a lot of fun with your loved ones while making dinner! The recipes in the Air Fryer Cookbook will help you prepare healthier versions of your old standbys without sacrificing any of the deliciousness. In addition to keeping your family healthy, you can also ensure they enjoy the food you provide. Put an end to worrying about the quality of food you serve your family. Without having to feel guilty about it later, you can continue to eat whatever tasty meals you like.

Those extra calories and fat from deep-fried foods aren't necessary any longer. An air fryer may produce equally appetizing results without the added oil and calories. We can finally enjoy tasty foods without feeling guilty. By following the instructions in The Air Fryer Cookbook, you can now prepare all the delicious food you love from a deep fryer with a fraction of the oil and calories. Now you may satisfy your appetite for the tasty fare while also satisfying your body's nutritional needs. For many years to come, your copy of The Air Fryer Cookbook will be a useful addition to your kitchen counter. It's time to get back to loving the kitchen; it's time to ditch the junk food and adopt a better diet. But don't feel like you have to stick to just the recipes in this book; branch out and try something new every now and then! Try out some other dishes. Don't be afraid to try new things in the kitchen. Develop some original dishes and have an open mind. In this way, you'll be able to get the most out of your air fryer.

Made in the USA
Middletown, DE
29 October 2022

13709292R00053